Godly Man

MEN in the Church

Steven B. Borst

CPH
SAINT LOUIS

Series editors: Thomas J. Doyle and Rodney L. Rathmann

This publication is also available in braille and in large print for the visually impaired. Write to Library for the Blind, 1333 S. Kirkwood Road, St. Louis, MO 63122-7295, or call 1-800-433-3954.

Copyright © 1998 Concordia Publishing House
3558 South Jefferson Avenue, St. Louis, MO 63118-3968
Manufactured in the United States of America

CONTENTS

Introduction

The Godly Man Series

In his letter to the recently established Christian church at Philippi, the apostle Paul likened the Christian life to a race. Paul wrote, "Forgetting what is behind and straining toward what is ahead, I press on toward the goal to win the prize for which God has called me heavenward in Christ Jesus" (Philippians 3:13–14).

Each of us who by faith claims Jesus as Lord and Savior has God's permission and His power to forget "what is behind." Over 2,000 years ago, Jesus came to earth, true God, Son of the eternal Father and yet true man. Conceived by the Holy Spirit and born of the Virgin Mary, Jesus grew as a boy—through childhood and adolescence—to become a mature man. He endured all the temptations and struggles every man has faced and yet committed no sin of thought, word, or action (Hebrews 4:14–15). According to His Father's plan, He suffered and died on the cross as our substitute, taking our sins upon Himself. We can forget our sins because Jesus' love has overcome our past. He has won the victory over our sins and the constraining, handicapping power of the devil. Jesus showed Himself Lord over sin, death, and the devil when He rose from the dead on Easter morning. We who believe in the crucified, risen, and ascended Savior are made new men by the same Holy Spirit who brought us to faith. As God's Spirit gives us new desires and a new set of goals and priorities, He changes us through the Word of God—the Gospel—so that we come to know God's love and the outpouring of His grace in mighty ways and grow in our relationship with our Father in heaven. Long ago, by inspiration of the Holy Spirit, the psalmist wrote the following insight into God and His nature, "His pleasure is not in the strength of the horse, nor His delight in the legs of a man; the LORD delights in those who fear Him, who put their hope in His unfailing love" (Psalm 147:10–11).

As we run life's race, our heavenly Father invites us to find our strength and encouragement in Him. His joy is not in any physical means by which men may reach a finish line, such as in the power of a horse or the legs of men. Rather God finds His joy in those sons who put their hope in Him and in the power of His unfailing love.

God's Word reminds us, "[We] are all sons of God through faith in Christ Jesus" (Galatians 3:26), and our God delights in His relationship with His sons just as every good father prides himself in the growth and accomplishments of his children. He invites us to communicate with Him regularly and often as we experience His Word and respond to His love in prayer.

As we press on toward our heavenly prize, God helps us live our lives for Him. Many of God's faithful people, both men and women, have lived before us. From them we receive a heritage to build on and to pass on to those who will follow after us—our wives, children, friends, and others whose lives will be touched by the love and power of God demonstrated in our lives.

The writer to the Hebrews encourages us to live as men of faith, reminding us about where to keep our focus as we run life's race: "Therefore, since we are surrounded by such a great cloud of witnesses, let us throw off everything that hinders and the sin that so easily entangles, and let us run with perseverance the race marked out for us. Let us fix our eyes on Jesus, the author and perfecter of our faith, who for the joy set before Him endured the cross, scorning its shame, and sat down at the right hand of the throne of God. Consider Him who endured such opposition from sinful men, so that you will not grow weary and lose heart" (Hebrews 12:1–3).

God's blessings as you run the race and claim the prize already won for you!

About the Godly Man Series

The Godly Man series is especially for men. Written in book-study format, each course in the Godly Man series is organized into chapters suitable for either group or individual study. Periodically throughout each chapter, questions have been provided to further stimulate your thinking, assist you in personal application, and spark group discussion.

How to Use Each Course in the Godly Man Series

Each course in the Godly Man series has been prepared especially for small group settings. It may, however, be used as a self-study or in a traditional Sunday morning Bible class. Chapters of each course may be read in advance of group discussion. Or participants may take turns reading sections of the Bible study during your group study sessions.

Planning for a Small Group Study

1. *Select a leader* for the course or a leader for the day. It will be the leader's responsibility to secure needed materials, to keep the discussion moving, and to help involve all participants.

2. *Emphasize sharing.* Your class will work best if the participants feel comfortable with one another and if all feel their contributions to the class are important and useful. Take the necessary time at the beginning of the course to get to know one another. Share what you expect to gain from this course. Develop an atmosphere of openness, trust, and caring among the participants. Agree in advance that private issues shared during your study will remain within the group.

3. *Pray for one another.* Begin and conclude each study session with a prayer. Pray for one another, for your families, your work, and all other aspects of your life. Involve everyone. Consider praying-around-the-circle, with each person offering a specific prayer to God for the person on his left.

As You Plan to Lead the Group

1. Read this guide in its entirety before you lead the first session.

2. Use the "Answers and Comments" section in the back of the study.

3. Pray each day for those in your group.

4. Depend on the Holy Spirit. Expect His presence; He will guide you and cause you to grow. God will not let His Word return empty (Isaiah 55:11) as you study it individually or with others in a group.

5. Prepare well, studying each session's material thoroughly. Add your comments in the margins so that you may add your insights to spark conversation and discussion throughout the session.

6. Begin and end the session with prayer.

7. Begin and end on time. Punctuality is a courtesy to everyone and can be a factor to encourage discussion.

8. Find ways to keep the session informal; consider meeting over breakfast at a local restaurant or some other friendly setting where participants can be seated face to face.

9. Keep the class moving. Limit your discussion to questions of interest to the participants. Be selective. You don't need to cover every question. Note that most Bible references are included in the Study Guide. At times, however, you may want to look up and share additional insights provided by other suggested Bible references.

10. Build one another up through your fellowship and study. Make a conscious effort to support one another in your personal and professional challenges.

Expect and rejoice in God's presence and blessing as He builds your faith and enriches your life through the study of His Word.

Worship:
The Most Important Hour in Your Week

Ready

Craig Olsen is president and CEO of Fresh Start Bakeries, Inc. He is also a member of Salem Lutheran Church in Orange, California. At an early Friday morning breakfast meeting over coffee, juice, and oatmeal, *Godly Man* queried Craig on how he juggles a demanding professional career with a vibrant worship life.

G.M.: What does the CEO of a bakery do?

Olsen: Fresh Start supplies McDonalds with all of its breads and rolls. This is probably over 95 percent of our business. I currently oversee 3 bakeries in the United States, and 14 bakeries in Europe and South America.

G.M.: How would you describe the demands of your job?

Olsen: McDonalds is a very demanding customer. The McDonalds culture has a high business ethic based on personal relationships, and therefore I find myself personally involved in all aspects of our relationship with them around the world. Because we have built such a solid tie with them, McDonalds also has me consult with other Latin American countries on how to do business with their franchise. This causes me to travel about 75 percent of my work week.

Ultimately, my first responsibility is to be the strategic leader of Fresh Start. We have seen such rapid growth over the last 15 years that we keep our organizational chart in pencil! I think we work so well with McDonalds because I make sure we protect our company culture. My Senior Vice President of Administration, for instance, is an ordained minister!

G.M.: I was going to ask you if you find it difficult being a Christian in corporate America. It sounds as if you've created an atmosphere in which you can follow your values.

Olsen: I actually left big business for a time over ethical concerns. I vowed at that time that I'd never go back again! In 1981, I was working as an officer for Fresh Start, and I had some serious differences of opinion with the CEO. I felt as if the way we were doing business was putting our relationship with McDonalds in jeopardy.

In 1982, Fresh Start hired me to be their new CEO partially because I was a Christian. They wanted me to set a new ethical standard. My premise was that you can be more successful financially if you run a corporation ethically. I think I've proven that's true over the long term.

G.M.: I know that you are one of the more regular Sunday worshipers at your church. With your schedule, how do you do it?

Olsen: I make it a top priority. Ninety percent of the time, I can make it to church. I engineer my schedule and take a firm stance to be home Sunday mornings. There's been more than one occasion when I've left for the airport right after worship was over.

G.M.: Are you ever tempted to sleep in?

Olsen: No. Worship is important to me and my family. I think it's critical to teach our children how important worship is. Skipping church is just not an option—it's part of our life. Church supplies us with meaningful time together as a family, and with my schedule, that's hard to engineer!

G.M.: Why is worship so important in your life?

Olsen: It's too easy to get involved with the details of life and forget about your relationship with God, which is more important. Worship is a discipline that brings me back to a spiritual reality. Every Sunday I return to ground zero and refocus. I also enjoy the personal connection with other Christians. There is spiritual safety in coming back to the "nest" before I venture out again. Part of your relationship with God is personal, but the other part happens in fellowship.

G.M.: Did you worship regularly as a child?

Olsen: I did. My father was a man with a big heart who was very involved in church. He died when I was only 14, but he made worship a priority in my life. It wasn't forced—just a part of our family culture.

G.M.: What's your favorite hymn or song?

Olsen: "Shine Jesus Shine." It's energizing!

G.M.: What benefits do you see in your life in worshiping together as a family?

Olsen: Shared faith is a part of our connection at the most basic level. Shared faith is shared strength. My second favorite song is "As for Me and My House, I Will Serve the Lord." This is how God intended it to be. Faith is personal, but faith is also a part of a family experience as designed by God. When God correlates Christ's relationship with the church to marriage, I mean, how could it be more clear? When I got married, I have to admit I couldn't articulate that, but I have seen over the years what a great gift worshiping together is.

G.M.: There will be men working through this book whose corporate life resembles yours. What would you say to them if they're feeling that adding regular worship to their day planners seems a monumental task?

Olsen: If you give it the priority in your life it deserves, it will become an effortless part of your life. Part of that is the work of the Holy Spirit. He makes it easy. Also, keep in mind that it's your responsibility as head of a family, and you need to lead by example. It's honestly something I don't think twice about.

REACT

1. Describe in your own words the role of worship in Craig's life.

2. If you were interviewed about the importance of worship in your life, what would you say?

Read

"Come On!"

Psalm 95 is one of the great calls to worship found in the Scriptures. Its first word, "Come," is translated into Latin as "Venite." Verses 1–7a have become known as the "Venite" and have been set to music for centuries in the church to be used as an opening for worship.

Come, let us sing for joy to the LORD;
    Let us shout aloud to the Rock of our salvation.
Let us come before Him with thanksgiving
    and extol Him with music and song.
For the LORD is the great God,
    the great King above all gods.
In His hand are the depths of the earth,
    and the mountain peaks belong to Him.
The sea is His, for He made it,
    and His hands formed the dry land.
Come, let us bow down in worship,
    let us kneel before the LORD our Maker;
for He is our God
    and we are the people of His pasture,
    the flock under His care.
Today, if you hear His voice,
    do not harden your hearts as you did at Meribah,
    as you did that day at Massah in the desert,
where your fathers tested and tried Me,
    though they had seen what I did.

For forty years I was angry with that generation;
    I said, "They are a people whose hearts go astray,
    and they have not known my ways."
So I declared an oath in My anger,
    "They shall never enter my rest." (Psalm 95)

REACT

1. How do verses 1–2 describe worship? Does this describe your last worship experience? Why or why not?

2. List the reasons the psalmist gives for worshiping God.

3. Verse 7a describes the unique relationship Christians have with God. Share an experience through which you discovered that you were part of "the flock under His care."

Read

But I'll Miss Sunday Morning Football!

The year? 1997. The team? The Green Bay Packers. The coach? Mike Holmgren. The result? First Super Bowl victory in 30 years.

When Mike was a child, there was rarely a Sunday when all three generations of Holmgrens weren't in worship. It was the most important hour of their week. As Mike grew up, however, his focus began to change. "My appetite for spiritual things was not so substantial as it is today; I was more interested in pickup games of touch football." By the time Mike Holmgren was a senior in high school, he was an all-American quarterback.

Mike's life came to the crossroads in 1970. Looking to go pro, he was given the chance of a lifetime: he was given a try-out to become the back-up quarterback to Joe Namath of the New York Jets. Mike gave it his best shot, but the Jets decided to go with a more experienced player. Mike Holmgren was crushed.

"All that had mattered to me was playing pro football, and now that would never happen. The flight home from New York was the longest five hours of my life. I felt like a failure. … In my pursuit to make a name for myself in football, I had left God on my bedroom shelf—right next to my dust-covered Bible. … I didn't know it at the time, but the shards of my broken dreams became the material that God used to shape my future."

That experience led Mike to open up his Bible. In it, he found new comfort and direction. In his study, Mike found Proverbs 3:5–6 to be an especially important passage for his life: "Trust in the LORD with all your heart, and lean not on your own understanding: in all your ways acknowledge Him, and He will make your paths straight." Mike began to live that passage, and the Lord led him into coaching at the collegiate level in the 1980s, and into the pros in the 1990s. By 1997, he had reached the pinnacle of his career.

Through it all, Mike Holmgren has learned why worship

is the most important hour in his week. "Win or lose, I now realize what really matters: It's not the Super Bowl rings— it's the crown of eternal life that Jesus Christ has won for us through his victory on the cross."

Adapted from Greg Asimakoupoulos, "What Matters Most in My Life," *Decision,* October 1997, pp. 8–9. Used by permission.

REACT

1. Have you or has someone you know had a "Mike Holmgren" experience? What happened that brought you/him/her back to the Lord?

2. The First Commandment forbids us to worship other "gods." In what ways are you tempted and/or coerced to worship the equivalent of a Super Bowl ring in your professional or personal life?

Read

Worship or Whine?

It seems easier to praise God when things are going well, but how about when life becomes chaotic, disappointing, and downright difficult? The end of Psalm 95 refers to such a time for the Israelites, "where your fathers tested and tried me" at Meribah and Massah. This episode took place after God had freed the Israelites from Egypt's tyranny and as He was leading them to the Promised Land. Along the way, would the Israelites worship or whine? Read about what happened in Exodus 17:1–7.

> The whole Israelite community set out from the Desert of Sin, traveling from place to place as the Lord commanded. They camped at Rephidim, but there was no water for the people to drink. So they quarreled with Moses and said, "Give us water to drink."
>
> Moses replied, "Why do you quarrel with me? Why do you put the LORD to the test?"
>
> But the people were thirsty for water there, and they grumbled against Moses. They said, "Why did you bring us up out of Egypt to make us and our children and livestock die of thirst?"
>
> Then Moses cried out to the LORD, "What am I to do with these people? They are almost ready to stone me."
>
> The LORD answered Moses, "Walk on ahead of the people. Take with you some of the elders of Israel and take in your hand the staff with which you struck the Nile, and go. I will stand there before you by the rock at Horeb. Strike the rock, and water will come out of it for the people to drink." So Moses did this in the sight of the elders of Israel. And he called the place Massah and Meribah because the Israelites quarreled and because they tested the LORD saying, "Is the LORD among us or not?"

React

1. Of what did the Israelites complain in verse 3? Considering their life as slaves in Egypt, why is their complaint ironic?

2. God promises that when we worship in His name He is present. How did the Israelites test God (verse 7)?

3. How do trials affect your relationship with God? How can they end up being times of "Meribah" (quarreling) and "Massah" (testing)?

4. Do you know anyone who continued to worship God regularly, even in the midst of suffering? If so, share the story.

Read

No Worship, No Rest

"If you hear His voice, do not harden your hearts," the psalmist warns us. In worship God's people come to hear His voice. God speaks to us in His Word. As we come into His presence, God provides us instruction, guidance, power, and grace.

Many men make all kinds of excuses not to worship regularly. They reason that Sunday mornings are their only morning to sleep in, or read the paper, or play tennis. They figure that they can just as easily worship God in the middle of a lake fishing than in the middle of a crowded pew. While it is true that we can interact with God throughout the week in devotions and prayer, God has set aside the Sabbath as a time for all His people to congregate and to receive from Him the forgiveness, power, and strength that come only from His Word.

The word "Sabbath" is Hebrew for rest. Worshiping God means resting in Him. God invites us to lay our heavy burdens of sin at the cross and receive forgiveness through Christ. He invites us to bring our worries and lift them up in prayer. Jesus, the Bread of Life, invites us to feast with Him at the table, where He offers us His true body and blood. In worship God gives us a type of rest that a hammock, garden chair, or golf cart could never give. By grace, God draws us into His presence. He provides us the opportunity to spend time with the One who created us.

Psalm 95 ends with a chilling pronouncement. To those who hear God's invitation to come into His presence, but harden their hearts, God says, "They shall never enter My rest." The chasing after life's delicacies will only lead to a life of restlessness. If you want true peace and rest in your crazy, imperfect life, then listen to the psalmist: "Come, let us bow down in worship, let us kneel before the Lord our Maker."

Respond

1. In Psalm 84, the psalmist makes an incredulous statement: "Better is one day in Your courts than a thousand elsewhere" (v. 10). How does the most important hour of our week affect the "thousand" hours around it?

2. Read Hebrews 10:19–25. Why can we persevere in faith and worship?

3. Beginning this week, make a commitment to worship regularly. If you are married, ask your wife to support you.

Being a Spiritual Leader at Home

Ready

What makes a good leader? Do you display the character-istics of a good leader? In the spaces provided below, list three significant leadership positions you've held in your life. Then list three key traits or skills you have found necessary to be a good leader.

Three Leadership Positions I Have Held	Three Keys to Good Leadership
1.	1.
2.	2.
3.	3.

REACT

Share your answers with your group. Then explore the following questions.

1. What are some common leadership roles among the men in your group? Do you think these are typical for most men? Why or why not?

2. Of all the key traits or skills mentioned, which do you think is the most important for a leader to possess? Why?

3. Have you had a male hero or mentor who has shown outstanding leadership? Who is he, and what made him such a great leader?

Read

Me, a Spiritual Leader?

We are all asked to take on many different types of leadership roles. Whether for a group at work, a committee at church, or as a coach for Little League, most men have had a variety of experiences as a leader. Whether we think about it or not, we are also in positions of leadership at home. You are probably at least partially responsible to be your family's breadwinner. You may also be in charge of paying the bills, manicuring the yard, or maintaining the cars. But have you ever considered yourself the spiritual leader of your family?

Many men have neglected God's calling to spiritual leadership. Our fathers may have been religious, but not openly so. As boys, we may have never heard our fathers pray out loud (except for the "Our Father" at church) or seen them reading the Scriptures, or sat at their feet while they told us the stories of Abraham, Isaac, and Jacob. Perhaps spiritual leadership in the home is something we've never really considered because we never experienced it.

Not that most Christian men don't take their faith seriously. Many try to observe the sacred hour regularly and have a private devotional life. Too few, though, have provided authentic spiritual leadership for their families. Instead, we too often have delegated this role to others in the church, who teach or catechize our kids for us. When Christian instruction is needed in the home, it is too easy for us to allow our wives to be responsible for making sure it gets done. Many men have not initiated significant spiritual experiences with their spouses, not because they are against such experiences, but rather because they've lacked the experiences that have taught them how to make it happen.

REACT

1. What kind of spiritual leadership did your father give when you were growing up?

2. How might you provide greater spiritual leadership in your family?

Read

A Guy Named Eli

Eli is an example of a man guilty of lackluster spiritual leadership in the home. Read how God finally confronts Eli through his apprentice Samuel in 1 Samuel 3:2–18.

React

1. Does God's judgment on Eli seem extreme? How might it be possible for a priest to neglect spiritual leadership in the home? Why do you think spiritual leadership is often difficult for men?

2. 1 Samuel 2:12 says, "Eli's sons were wicked men; they had no regard for the LORD." If you have children, do they have regard for the Lord? How can you positively influence their faith life and faith development?

3. Read Deuteronomy 6:4–9. How serious does God consider the role of spiritual leadership?

Read

Taking the Right Passage

Richard Rohr, OFM, is the author of several books on men's spirituality, including *The Wild Man's Journey* (St. Anthony Messenger Press, 1992) and *The Quest for the Grail* (Crossroad, 1994). His expertise focuses on the rites of passage through which people go to become healthy spiritual adults. Rohr finds that such rites of passage are often vague. Frequently children do not have a parent to lead them through these important transitions in life. In a 1998 article in *Sojourners* magazine, Rohr makes these comments about the lack of spiritual leadership and the vacuum it has created:

> In a deconstructing culture, there is nothing to initiate a young man into except perhaps his private male sensibility. ... Coaches and drill sergeants, smoking and driving, money and merit badges, graduation and girlfriends have become our only mentors and rites of passage. ... What we have in post-Vietnam America is an entire country of older men falsely initiated into militarism and materialism, middle-aged men who were swindled of their only shot at significance, and many sad young men who do not believe that there are any sacred mysteries to be initiated into! No wonder we are deconstructing. We do not know what to do with our pain, and we know that most of our power is pseudo and worthless.

From "Boys to Men," Richard Rohr, OFM, *Sojourners*, May-June 1998, pp. 17–21. Reprinted with permission from *Sojourners*, 2401 15th St. NW, Washington, DC 20009; 1-800-714-7474.

So what might spiritual leadership in the home look like? Men must first realize that their calling is not just to be taskmasters of morality. Ephesians 6:4 says "Fathers, do not exasperate your children; instead bring them up in the training and instruction of the Lord." While good behavior is always a "work-in progress" for Christians, Christianity is much more than just being good. Instructing our daughters and sons about the Lord means telling them about the forgiveness that Jesus Christ has won for them on the cross. It means showing them their new identity by virtue of their

Baptism into Jesus, that they are not just our children, but more important, God's children.

What sort of leadership traits are needed to be an effective spiritual leader at home? Some of the traits you listed in the "Ready" exercise at the beginning of this session will be applicable, but there is an added trait, which more than likely wasn't on your list at all, that is important: being vulnerable. In our vulnerability, we find a powerful resource to teach our children the Gospel: we are able to show them that we, too, are sinners in need of repentance and God's undeserved love. This vulnerability is most important when life is difficult and doesn't make sense. A spiritual leader provides his family the opportunity to speak their doubts and worries by showing them the underside of his own soul where worry and doubt reside. He then gives direction to turn once again to God's Word for comfort and wisdom. A spiritual leader doesn't just ask for others to pray, or serve, or read a family devotion. A spiritual leader himself prays, serves, and reads. Our best leadership comes when we become vulnerable and live out our faith with and in front of our families.

Perhaps the best teaching on authentic spiritual leadership comes when the Bible instructs men about their relationship to their wives. In doing so, it paints a portrait of Jesus' relationship to the church. "Husbands, love your wives, just as Christ loved the church and gave Himself up for her" (Ephesians 5:25). To be the spiritual head of the house is not to lord it over our wives, but to love them with the love Jesus has first showed us. Through faith, spiritual leaders sacrifice themselves for the benefit of their families.

Respond

Richard Rohr concludes his comments on being a spiritual mentor for our families with this statement: "Finally, you can only give away what you have. If fathers have not gone through significant spiritual passages themselves, they really have nothing to say to the young men." Spiritual leadership must find its source in the Holy Spirit, for if we ourselves are malnourished, our leadership will be frail, too.

Take time this week to be strengthened in your own

faith, and take a new step in leadership in your home. Choose one item from the list below to enact this week.

My Faith My Leadership

1. I will learn more about prayer by studying Luke 11:1–11 this week. I will pray with my wife this week.

2. I will learn more about struggling with sin by reading Romans 7:7–8:4. I will share what I've learned with my child(ren) or spouse.

3. I will learn more about how God works through my struggles in 1 Peter 1:3–21. I will set aside a time to talk about struggles we have as a family, and I will pray that God will strengthen our faith.

4. Other:

Real Men Pray

3

Ready

Ephesians 6:12 says, "For our struggle is not against flesh and blood, but against the rulers, against the authorities, against the powers of this dark world and against the spiritual forces of evil in the heavenly realms." If we could see with our own eyes what is described in that verse, what would it look like? Further, how does this struggle connect with the injunction that follows in verse 18? "And pray in the Spirit on all occasions with all kinds of prayers and requests. With this in mind, be alert and always keep on praying for all the saints."

Frank Peretti wrote several fictional books specifically to explore these questions. In *Piercing the Darkness*, Sally Beth Roe is a young woman living in a small town called Bacon's Corner. She finds herself in the middle of a murder case, continually harassed and misled by the demonic! The demons' stronghold is the Summit Institute, a gathering place of New Age philosophers involved in pagan and satanic rituals. In the excerpt below, Christians from the town of Ashton have been praying for Sally, and the Lord's angels are planning her rescue from the spiritual forces of evil.

"Captain Tal!" came a shout. A courier dropped from the sky like a meteor, snapping his wings open just in time to alight directly in front of Tal. "Mota sends word from Bacon's Corner! The prayers have brought a breakthrough! They've opened the breach, sir! They're ready to expose Broken Birch!"

Tal laughed with excitement. "Well enough! The kindling is stacked, and"—he looked at Sally—"we now have the match to start the brushfire! Nathan and Armoth!"

"Captain!" they replied.

"Sally's ready. Follow her from here on, and be sure Krioni and Triskal are warned to secure Ashton from invasion. When she lights the brushfire, sound the signal for Mota and Signa in Bacon's Corner."

29

"Done!"

Tal turned to the courier. "Tell Mota and Signa that they have the prayer cover and can proceed closing the trap. After that, have them wait for the signal from Nathan and Armoth."

The courier flew off with the message.

Tal put a brotherly hand on Guilo's shoulder. "Guilo, the Strength of Many, it's time to position the armies at the Summit Institute!"

"YAHAAA!" Guilo roared, raising his sword for the other warriors to see. "Done!"

Tal unfurled his wings with the sound of a crashing ocean wave. He raised his sword high, and they all did the same so that Lakeland Park was flooded with the flickering light. "For the saints of God and for the Lamb!"

Excerpt from *Piercing the Darkness* by Frank Peretti, © 1989. Used by permission of Crossway Books, a division of Good News Publishers, Wheaton, Illinois.

Read

Take a Breather!

While the Bible does not tell us that our prayers actually provide "cover" for the angels to do their work, God's Word does make it clear that prayer is one of our greatest weapons in spiritual warfare. Prayer is vitally important to our spiritual life, so much so that one of the ancient church fathers described prayer as the way a Christian breathes.

No character in the Bible better depicts the importance of "Christian breath" than Daniel. He exemplifies our axiom that "Real Men Pray." Read his story in Daniel 6:1–23.

React

1. How often did Daniel pray? Why?

2. While Daniel's predicament seems extreme, it is not farfetched. Even today, Christians in various parts of the world risk their very lives to worship God. If the death penalty were instituted for those who prayed, would you continue to do so? If so, when, where, and how would you pray?

3. What forces do you face that intimidate you from praying boldly, regularly, and/or publicly?

Read

Of First Importance

Is prayer for the Christian man often just an afterthought? Perhaps this is the case because men in our culture are taught to be self-reliant. Our immediate reaction to roadblocks in our lives is to find a way around them. Prayer becomes a last resort, a sign of weakness and failure.

Scripture teaches exactly the opposite. With such imperatives as "pray continually" (1 Thessalonians 5:17), "Ask, and it will be given to you" (Matthew 7:7), "Is any of you in trouble? He should pray" (James 5:13), and "in everything, by prayer and petition, with thanksgiving, present your requests to God" (Philippians 4:6), God encourages us to use prayer not as a last resort, but as of first importance.

Prayer calls us again to faith, for in prayer, we are made mindful of our reliance on the Father. He gives all things physical and spiritual to meet our every care. Indeed, Jesus teaches us that "when you pray, do not keep on babbling like pagans, for they think they will be heard because of their many words ... Your Father knows what you need before you ask Him" (Matthew 6:7–8). Prayer, therefore, has a reciprocal effect: it is the means by which we communicate our inmost thoughts to God, and at the same time, it reminds us of our complete dependence on God's gracious response to our needs.

Read

Sometimes It's the Only Solution

Have you ever heard the statement "All we can do now is pray"? When is this usually spoken? When we find ourselves in precarious predicaments (such as the serious illness of a loved one), we are literally reduced to the "Christian's breath." In those instances do we use prayer as a whimper or a weapon?

Moses and Aaron were real men who prayed with power and purpose. Read of one particular instance in Exodus 17:8–16 when their very lives depended on it!

React

1. Do you think it was a wise use of manpower to keep Moses and Aaron out of the din of battle? Do you think the soldiers in the field felt this way?

2. What connection was there between Moses' lifting up holy hands in prayer and the success of his troops?

3. Describe Aaron's role.

4. Describe an instance when your only hope was prayer. How did you feel? Do you tire easily from praying regularly?

Read

Where Do I Start?

If you have never had an active prayer life, or haven't had one in a while, trying to start talking to God can be as uncomfortable as making dinner conversation with people you've just met. What should we pray? How long and how often? How should I address God? Should I keep a list of prayer requests? All these and more are issues you will face as a man of prayer.

In Luke 11, the disciples of Jesus felt just as uncomfortable with their prayer life as we sometimes do. Feeling frustrated, they finally dropped all pretenses and just came right out and asked Jesus how to do it.

> One day Jesus was praying in a certain place. When He finished one of His disciples said to Him, "Lord, teach us to pray, just as John taught his disciples."
> He said to them, "When you pray, say:
> 'Father, hallowed be Your name,
> Your kingdom come.
> Give us each day our daily bread.
> Forgive us our sins,
> for we also forgive everyone who sins against us.
> And lead us not into temptation.'"
> (Luke 11:1–4)

Read

Jesus' Prayer

Jesus' prayer has been recited verbatim since the beginning of His church. What we overlook, however, is that this prayer is not only worthy of recitation, but it also is a useful guide and outline for our own prayers.

Notice how Jesus teaches us to address God: "Father." St. Paul goes so far as to tell us we can call Him "Abba," which means "daddy." While prayers said in a public worship service often lean toward the formal, our own private prayers can be intimate discourses between us and our Father. We can trust the One with whom we speak, for He is the perfect Father, who loves us unconditionally and delights in spending time with us.

As Jesus gets into the content of prayer, notice for whom we are first instructed to pray: God! We pray for God's name, kingdom, and in Matthew's version of the Lord's Prayer, God's will to be done on earth as it is in heaven. Whether we pray these petitions or not, God's name is holy, His kingdom will come, and His will does take place. What we ask for, then, is that these things would happen in our lives, personally! In essence, Jesus teaches us to pray for a more profound relationship with God.

The rest of the prayer deals with our daily needs and the needs of those around us. We are told to pray for the mundane (bread includes all food, shelter, clothing) and that which deals with the immortal, the forgiveness of sins. Jesus invites us to speak to Him about everything! Nothing is too great for God to handle, nor too small for Him to care.

Read and React

Jesus' Prayer Life

In her book *Jesus, Man of Prayer*, Margaret Magdalene examines the prayer life of Jesus Christ. It is a fascinating look at how prayer permeated our Lord's life and how He prayed at various times and in various ways. Below is a list of some of the forms that Jesus' prayers took. Examine each of them to see how often you pray in these different ways, and respond with the following scale:

1—Never   2—Rarely   3—Sometimes   4—Often   5—Consistently

Jesus' Prayers

_____ 1. Praying to the Father intimately: "When you pray, pray 'Abba.' " (Luke 11:2).

_____ 2. Praying liturgically: "And He went on the Sabbath day into the synagogue, as was His custom" (Luke 4:16).

_____ 3. Praying through the Scriptures: "Hear God's Word and put it into practice" (Luke 8:21).

_____ 4. Praying on behalf of others: "I have prayed for you, Simon, that your faith may not fail" (Luke 22:31,32).

_____ 5. Praying in desolation: "My God, why have You forsaken Me?" (Matthew 27:46).

_____ 6. Being ready to pray: "Watch and pray so that you will not fall into temptation." (Mark 14:38)

_____ 7. Praying through the senses, in response to creation: "See how the lilies of the field grow" (Matthew 6:28).

Adapted from *Jesus, Man of Prayer* by Margaret Magdalene. © 1987 Inter-Varsity Press. Used by permission.

Read

Jesus Makes Prayer Work

As we begin to talk to God on a regular basis, we will gain confidence in praying. We will begin to feel more and more open in sharing everything with Him. Yet, God does not listen and respond to our prayers because they are eloquent, or even because we're giving it our best effort. On the contrary, Romans 8:26 says, "We do not know what we ought to pray for, but the Spirit Himself intercedes for us with groans that words cannot express." Our confidence in prayer, therefore, can't rely on our own abilities. There must be a greater source for confidence in our prayer life: Jesus Himself.

Therefore, since we have a great high priest who has gone through the heavens, Jesus the Son of God; let us hold firmly to the faith we profess. For we do not have a high priest who is unable to sympathize with our weaknesses, but we have one who has been tempted in every way, just as we are—yet was without sin. Let us then approach the throne of grace with confidence, so that we may receive mercy and find grace to help us in our time of need. (Hebrews 4:14–16)

When Jesus Christ died on the cross for the world, He opened up a highway to heaven that had previously been shut down. Jesus was perfect, without sin, and therefore was the perfect offering for our sins. At the cross, the perfect Son of God took on all our imperfections and paid for them with His life. The benefit of this work is that we are forgiven. No longer does our sin and rebellion against God need to cut off our relationship with Him. Through faith in Jesus, we can confidently walk into the Father's throne room and boldly tell Him what's on our mind. We can trust that God will answer our prayers, not because of anything we've done, but because of what Jesus has done for us.

Respond

1. Look above at Margaret Magdalene's list of different ways Jesus prayed. Choose one form for which you answered 1, 2, or 3, and work to include this form of prayer in your own prayer life.

2. Memorize this Scripture passage: "The prayer of a righteous man is powerful and effective" (James 5:16). Write it on a note card and put in a place that you will see it every day.

3. Steven Curtis Chapman is a Christian artist. In his *Sign of Life* album, he sings a song called "Let Us Pray."

> I hear you say your heart is aching
> You've got trouble in the making
> And you ask if I'll be praying for you please
> And in keeping with convention
> I'll say with good intentions
> To pray later making mention of your needs

But since we have this moment here at heaven's door
We should start knocking now, what are we waiting for?

Let us pray, let us pray, everywhere in every way
Every moment of the day, it is the right time
For the Father above, He is listening with love
And He wants to answer us, so let us pray.

From *"Let Us Pray"* by Steven Curtis Chapman, © 1996. Sparrow Song/Peach Hill Songs administered by EMI Music Pubishing. Used by permission.

STRENGTHENING
and Supporting One Another

4

Ready

You are a 35-year-old manager of an up and coming, but still struggling, computer firm. You are working on a shoe-string budget to create your own market share in a very competitive market. Your staff is meager, but very committed. They are mostly single, 20-something computer whizzes, who for six months have been working long hours and weekends to keep the company going.

You have recently hired a 37-year-old woman, who is an experienced computer marketing executive. She is also a single mother who gets no assistance from the dad of her child. As a new employee, she has worked hard, but can work no more than 60 hours per week, which is significantly less than any other employee. Because of this, other employees are starting to grumble. Since she hasn't been able to finish her assignments, some of her projects are behind.

This morning a supervisor has come to you and requested you let this new executive go. As you consider the request, you are torn. On the one hand, you don't want anyone to compromise the profitability of the company or the morale of the workforce. On the other hand, your company's literature boasts that it provides a "family-friendly" work environment.

Adapted from Joseph L. Badaracco Jr., *Defining Moments: When Managers Must Choose between Right and Right*, © 1997 Harvard Business School Press.

REACT

1. This fictional scenario is given as an ethical example in the book *Defining Moments*. Put yourself in the above quandary. What should you do?

2. Have you found yourself in the situation where strengthening and supporting someone might not be in the best interest of the group? What happened?

3. The book's author, Joseph L Badaracco Jr., suggests that the manager has sunk his own ship. He should have never hired the woman in the first place and ultimately looked weak to his own superiors by not dealing with an "inefficient" employee firmly. Badaracco suggests that the manager should fire the woman executive immediately. What do you think of this advice?

Read

A Story on Strengthening

"On one occasion an expert in the Law asked Jesus, 'What must I do to inherit eternal life?' " (Luke 10:25–27). Jesus led him to this answer: "Love the Lord your God with all your heart and with all your soul and with all your strength and with all your mind" and "Love your neighbor as yourself." Now the first part the man understood well enough: salvation comes through faith in God alone. We are to love, trust, and fear Him above all things. The second part, however, was a bit more difficult to swallow. In response to God's love for us in Christ Jesus, we love those around us.

The expert in the Law knew he had fallen short in loving others, but to make himself look good, he came up with a brilliant idea: "What if I specifically identify those whom I am to love? If I lessen the sphere of responsibility, I am more likely able to fulfill my role in supporting and strengthening others." In reply, Jesus offered him the parable found in Luke 10:30–37. Read the parable now.

REACT

1. Jews hated the Samaritans, whom they considered to be inferior, theologically incorrect hoodlums. If Jesus were telling this story today, what person do you think He would have chosen to rescue the man on the side of the road?

2. There is a connection between God's love for us and our love for others. Jesus told His disciples, "By this all men will know that you are My disciples, if you love one another" (John 13:35). What occurs when Christians (priests and Levites in the story) shirk their opportunities to support others?

3. What excuses do we make for ourselves when we pass by those in need?

Read

No "I" in Body

In the early 1990s, the University of Michigan boasted what many commentators believed to be the top five basketball players in the country. This quintessential quintet was quickly dubbed the "Fab Five," and talk of four successive NCAA championships dominated the sports section of newspapers. History, however, proved otherwise. While great superstars in their own right, they never meshed as a team. None of the "Fab Five" ever won one championship throughout their entire college careers.

St. Paul faced a similar situation in the city of Corinth. The church he started there was deeply divided by strife and jealousy. Those blessed with certain spiritual gifts felt superior to those whose gifts seemed more "average." Others acted in blatant disregard to those around them, oblivious to the effect their words and actions had on other people. Through spiritual selfishness, the church at Corinth became a chaotic mess.

It is for this reason that Paul wrote his letter to the Corinthians. In it, he calls them back to loving God—the God who loved them first in Jesus—with their whole hearts, and strengthening and supporting their neighbors as themselves. He drills his point home by using a mystical analogy for the church: we are the body of Christ. There is no "I" in the word "body!"

Read 1 Corinthians 12:12–27.

Read

Give Them Bread This Day

Baptized into Jesus Christ means not only that we have communion with God, but also that we are connected in a profound way to others whom God has called to faith in Jesus. To call other Christians "brothers and sisters" is really no exaggeration. Through Holy Baptism God adopted us as His children. Through faith all Christians are family. Galatians 6:10 puts it this way: "Therefore, as we have opportunity, let us do good to all people, especially to those who belong to the family of believers."

Brian Coleman was 15 years old in 1987. In that year he learned firsthand what Galatians 6:10 was all about. He attended a church youth group meeting in which the Bible study centered on the problem of poverty and hunger and how Christians desire to respond to those in need. The lesson really hit home when Brian and his friends left the meeting to go home for dinner. Right outside of the church, sleeping on the parish steps, was a homeless man. Coleman and his buddies pooled their money and bought the man some fast food. "He was clearly down on his luck, and he thanked us for the food," Coleman remembers.

Later that summer this teenage boy challenged his church to start a soup kitchen. Brian helped solicit 100 volunteers to man the kitchen and asked for donations from church members to pay for the food. The first night, they served five people. Today they serve over 150 people per week. A decade and one year later, Brian Coleman was ordained as a deacon in the Episcopal Church. At the end of his ordination ceremony, Brian gave this blessing to the congregation: "Let us go forth into the world, rejoicing in the power of the spirit!"

Adapted from "Feeding the Soul," *Los Angeles Times*, 14 June 1998, pp. B 1 and 3. Copyright 1998 Los Angels Times. Reprinted by permission.

React

1. The American ethic is to do for yourself; we are an individualistic people. Does Paul's teaching that there is no

"I" in the "body of Christ" set us at odds with attitudes of our society? How much "retraining" do Christians need to begin to think in terms of group, team, and church?

2. St. Paul really gives two reasons why people feel disconnected from the body of Christ. The first reason is described in 1 Corinthians 12:14–20, and the second in verses 21–26. How would you summarize these reasons, and which best describes you?

3. From the list that follows, which most accurately describes your church fellowship? How would you grade your church in regard to living together as the body of Christ? What tendencies do you see in your congregation to make you answer this way?
- We are unconnected Christians.
- We are friendly after worship.
- We are starting to make more meaningful relationships.
- We focus on strengthening and supporting one another.

4. Every congregation has one or more members who are always available to those in need. Share the story of one such person in your congregation.

Read

The Full Extent of God's Love

Before leaving His disciples, Jesus felt He had one more important lesson to teach His followers. It was the evening of Maundy Thursday, and Jesus and the disciples had journeyed into Jerusalem to celebrate the Passover. As they sat together in a second story room, Jesus taught them what supporting and strengthening one another was all about. Read John 13:1–17.

Read

How Do You Spell "Servant"?

It was customary that the task of washing a guest's feet fell to a house slave. Since Jesus and the disciples had borrowed the Upper Room, however, they were alone with no one to serve them. Jesus humbled Himself to become the servant of the house.

This type of servanthood shocked Peter. People of importance like Jesus (and like Peter, for that matter) didn't bother themselves with the details of other people's lives. Washing feet was someone else's job. Certainly they could hire someone else to do it for them, or at least one of the lesser disciples should be told to do the job. That Jesus would wash feet embarrassed Peter, for the thought of doing such a gesture himself never crossed Peter's mind. Jesus responds to Peter's objections with the words, "Unless I wash you, you have no part of Me."

Peter's story is our story. The fact that God would humble Himself to become a servant makes us feel uncomfortable. Yet Jesus states His mission clearly: "The Son of Man did not come to be served, but to serve, and to give His life as a ransom for many" (Matthew 20:28). Unless Jesus serves us, we cannot be a part of Him. Our superior rank among men does not warrant membership in His family. The only possible way for people to be associated with God is through the servant Jesus. This He accomplished through His death on the cross. On the cross, Jesus did much more than just wash our feet; He washed our "hands and head as well!" Christ was crucified to cleanse us of our sins and make us members of His body, the church!

Jesus serves us and through His service enables us to support and strengthen one another. He equips us to serve and gives us an example of how to do so. "Now that you know these things, you will be blessed if you do them."

Respond

1. One way that Jesus supported and strengthened the disciples was to mentor them. Consider mentoring a younger man at work or church.

2. Do you need to be strengthened and supported? Have you kept people away because of wanting to appear self-sufficient? Allow the body of Christ to nurture you.

3. How did you grade your congregation in the last "React" section? Find one way in which you might help make your congregation more caring.

Honoring God
with Time, Talents, and Treasures

Ready

People complain about time. They say that there is never enough time, that time is too short, and that time flies. Inflexible tasks, such as showering, commuting, working, sleeping, and eating, take up the bulk of our 168-hour week. Yet, once you subtract all these things, most men find that they still have anywhere between 30 to 50 hours of "disposable time" each week.

In the pie chart below, list four to six things you do that make up the biggest part of your disposable time. For any time left over, create a final slice to your graph and label it "Other." Use the following formula to determine how much time your chart represents:

40- to 50-hour work week = 50 hours of disposable time

50- to 60-hour work week = 40 hours of disposable time

60-plus-hour work week = 30 hours of disposable time

Disposable Time

Read

It's about Time

On the first day of creation, God said, "Let there be light," and with that there was the very first day and night. In other words, time as we know it began that day. While we may feel "confined" by a 24-hour day (especially since we know that in heaven we'll live outside the limits of time), God created time as part of His master plan for the universe. At the end of the first day, He declared, "This is good!"

Our time is a gift from God. In the Psalms we're told, "This is the day the LORD has made," therefore "let us rejoice and be glad in it" (Psalm 118:24). What do you do with this gift God has given? Do you use it to honor Him with hard work, healthy recreation, and service to others? Unfortunately, we know that too often our "timing" is not always so great, and we often waste time without even thinking about it.

Over and over again, the Bible beckons us to make better use of our time. In our prayers, we can include this petition: "Teach us to number our days aright, that we may gain a heart of wisdom" (Psalm 90:12). St. James warns us, "Now listen, you who say, 'Today or tomorrow we will go to this or that city, spend a year there, carry on business and make money.' Why, you do not even know what will happen tomorrow. What is your life? You are a mist that appears for a little while and then vanishes" (James 4:13–14). Paul urges: "Be very careful, then, how you live—not as unwise but as wise, making the most of every opportunity" (Ephesians 5:15).

Read

The Time Is Right

Jesus once told a parable about people who didn't have time for Him. Read it in Luke 14:15–24.

React

1. What sort of things preoccupied the invited guests? What sort of things crowd out your time to honor God?

2. Read Galatians 4:4–5. Describe God's timing and its effects on your life. How does knowledge of this timing affect your timing?

3. Imagine for a moment that an entire 80-year life span were reduced to 24 hours. At 6:00 A.M. a man would be 20 years old, 40 years old at noon, and 60 years old at 6:00 P.M. In what hour of the day are you? What can you expect from the rest of your "day?" What do you want to accomplish before your "day" is over?

Read

Show Talent

A second gift from God is the talents He gives us. Talents make us who we are. From our personality to our likes and dislikes, from our abilities to our experiences, God has gifted each one of us in a unique way. As with the gift of time, we are responsible for how we use our unique talents. What message does Jesus give us concerning honoring God with our talents in the Parable of the Talents found in Matthew 25:14–30?

Rᴇᴀᴄᴛ

1. Why did the third man in Jesus' parable bury his talents? What are some reasons you have been tempted at times not to use or to hide your talents?

2. Describe an instance when God has used you to perform a particular task. What gifts did He give you to accomplish it? What experiences prepared you for the job?

Rᴇᴀᴅ

Yᴏᴜ'ʀᴇ ᴛʜᴇ Mᴀɴ ꜰᴏʀ ᴛʜᴇ Jᴏʙ!

Have you ever been in a crisis situation when everyone in the room (or car, or field) turned to you for help? At that moment, you alone had the know-how to get the job done. That moment describes what God desires of our whole lives. God has gifted each of us uniquely because He values us and because He has particular tasks for each of us to accomplish.

Think for a moment about God's love for you. He not only

knows you by name and has saved you through the gift of His Son, but He also has a plan for your life. Ephesians 2:8–10 describes God's great love for you this way:

> For it is by grace you have been saved, through faith—and this not from yourselves, it is the gift of God—not by works, so that no one can boast. For we are God's workmanship, created in Christ Jesus to do good works, which God has prepared in advance for us to do. (Ephesians 2:8–10)

To you more than anyone else, God has given the right mix of talents to get done the jobs given to us by the Lord!

To steer us away from neglecting, abusing, or selfishly misusing our talents, Richard Rohr brings our life as a baptized Christian into focus with these words:

> Your life is not about you. This is the essential and summary experience. You must know that you are a part of something and somebody much bigger than yourself. Your life is not about you, it is about God. Henceforward, the entire human experience takes on a dramatically different character. We call it holiness.

From Richard Rohr, OFM, "Boys to Men," *Sojourner,* May—June 1998. Reprinted with permission from *Sojourners*, 2401 15th St. NW, Washington, DC 20009, 1-800-714-7474.

Read

Gimme!

The third "T" of God's great gifts to each of us is "treasures." Treasures represent our cash and worldly goods. In a final parable about honoring God, often called the Parable of the Rich Fool, Jesus warns us against selfishly hoarding what we have. Read the parable in Luke 12:13–21.

React

1. Why did God accuse the rich man of being a "fool?"

2. How have you at times foolishly used the "treasures" God has given you?

3. How has God enabled you to be rich toward Him (Luke 12:21)? See also 2 Timothy 3:14–17. How do the riches you have received through faith in Christ Jesus—forgiveness of sins and eternal life—enable you to use the treasures God has given you?

Read

Owner or Manager?

Perhaps you've been involved in a stewardship program at your church. At the end of many stewardship programs, members of the congregation are asked to pledge their donation to the church for the coming year. In doing so, members are encouraged to be good stewards of their treasures. What does the word "steward" mean?

Stewards are not owners, but managers. Stewardship calls us to manage faithfully what God has given us.

The difference between these two terms makes a world of

difference! When we act as masters of our own money, then we are merely doing God a favor when we choose to honor Him with it. The Bible, however, teaches us that God ultimately supplies us with all things. He has given us our days and our ability to work. He blesses us with health and has caused our labor to produce wealth. When we honor God with our treasures, therefore, we actually give back to Him what He has first given us! "Bring your burnt offerings and sacrifices, your tithes and special gifts, what you have vowed to give and your freewill offerings, and the firstborn of your herds and flocks," says Deuteronomy 12:6–7, "... because the LORD your God has blessed you."

When people inquire of your philanthropy, do they ask the question "What charities did you give to this year?" Did you ever stop to notice that the question is wrongly phrased? Using your treasures to bless God and His people is not a giving *to*, but rather giving *from*. We give from the abundance that God has stored up for us. We also give from a thankful heart that praises God for His generosity in supplying us with all that we need in this life and the next. Again, the book of Deuteronomy declares, "No man should appear before the LORD empty-handed: Each of you must bring a gift in proportion to the way the LORD your God has blessed you" (Deuteronomy 16:17).

John Wesley knew exactly what it meant to give *from*. Wesley, who founded the Methodist church, had one of the highest earned incomes in all of 18th-century England. Unlike the rich fool of whom Jesus spoke, when Wesley died, he was all but penniless. When it came to money, Wesley lived by this dictum: "Earn all you can, save all you can, then give all you can!"

From Andrea Neal, "Time Spent Agonizing over Money," *The Saturday Evening Post,* January/February 1998, p. 16.

God has called us to this kind of faith. "Remember this: Whoever sows sparingly will also reap sparingly, and whoever sows generously will also reap generously. Each man should give what he has decided in his heart to give, not reluctantly or under compulsion, for God loves a cheerful giver. And God is able to make all grace abound to you, so that in all things at all times, having all that you need, you will abound in every good work" (2 Corinthians 9:6–8).

REACT

1. On the continuum place an X to describe your giving. Then explain the reason for your response.

To _____ FROM

2. How does the proportion you give compare to the blessings the Lord has provided to you?

3. Our unwillingness to give back to the Lord that which He has given us is sin. For this and all other sins Jesus went to the cross to die. How will the richness of Jesus' love motivate you to give back to Him?

Respond

1. Refer back to the opening exercise on disposable time. Which one valuable use of time that doesn't currently appear on your pie chart would you like to include? Carve out some time in your day planner this week to honor God in this way.

2. 1 Peter 4:10 says, "Each one should use whatever gift he has received to serve others, faithfully administering God's grace in its various forms." What gifts has God given you? How might you better use those gifts to serve Him?

3. Write the following phrase on an index card, and put it on your refrigerator:

> "The fear of need, when the pantry is full, is the thirst that is unquenchable." —Kahlil Gibran

Living a Life of Witness

6

Ready

The fact that Jay Smith is a missionary isn't what makes him unique. It's how Jay evangelizes that sets him apart. Jay lives in England, and his specific assignment is to reach out to Muslims. On any given day of the week, you can find Jay openly confronting Muslims, either perched from a ladder at Speaker's Corner in Hyde Park or behind a podium in a highly publicized public debate.

Smith realized that working in England offered some definite advantages. "In the Islamic world you can not criticize the Qur'an nor the prophet or you would find yourself on the next plane home. ... Yet England and the U.S. are not hostile environments. The criteria needed for communicating the Gospel in the Muslim world are not relevant for England or for the West."

"Many have questioned the method that I and others are using in England to evangelize Muslims. They say it is wrong, perhaps even dangerous. ... In fact, the limits we place upon ourselves—to not be critical or confrontational—are not practiced by our Muslim friends. It is rare that a Muslim, while in dialogue with a Christian, fails to remind us that our Bible is not only corrupt but that our Lord is nothing more than a man. ... Then why do we choose to censor ourselves?"

Smith says he bases his approach both on Jesus' and St. Paul's methodologies. They too, he claims, openly debated with unbelievers. While this can be unsettling, Smith reminds Christians that "the good news is that we do have evidence for what we believe. ... Those who have gone before us were prepared to die for what they believed. Are we likewise prepared? I think it is only right that we take the challenge before us and follow their example."

Adapted from Jay Smith, "Courage in Our Convictions." *EMQ*, January 1998, pp. 28–35. Used by permission from *EMIS*, P.O. Box 794, Wheaton, IL 60189.

REACT

1. Think of an unchurched friend or acquaintance. Would Jay Smith's approach work with your friend? Why or why not?

2. Have you ever found yourself in a situation in which you've had to defend what you believe? What happened? How did that experience make you feel?

READ

TO BE OR NOT TO BE ... A WITNESS

Television shows like "Candid Camera" are built on the fact that it is interesting and often funny to spy on people and see how they respond in a controlled environment. If you think about it, we do this informally all the time. Whether we're waiting in a checkout lane, at a stoplight, or in an airport, we tend to "people watch." We're curious how they'll act in certain situations, especially if we think they don't see us peering at them out of the corner of our eye. The way they act and speak tell about who they are and what they believe.

Now comes the scary part: people peer at us all the time. It may be a stranger on the golf course, but more likely it's our neighbor or the employee at work. Whether we know it or not, we give a constant testimony of who we are and what we believe. While many Christian men find it difficult to witness their faith, what they don't realize is that their silence in things spiritual is a testimony, too—probably one which they don't mean to give!

We are witnesses whether we like it or not, not only because other people are watching us, but also more importantly because Christ has called us to witness. "You will be My witnesses," Jesus said, "in Jerusalem, and in all Judea and Samaria, and to the ends of the earth" (Acts 1:8). God, who could have engineered a lot of different ways to reveal Himself to humanity, has chosen us to be His spokespersons. St. Paul concludes, "It is written: 'I believed; therefore I have spoken.' With that same spirit of faith we also believe and therefore speak" (2 Corinthians 4:13). Being a Christian means being a witness.

REACT

In his book, *Overcoming Barriers to Witnessing,* Delos Miles identifies some barriers that diminish our witness. Read these barriers below, and circle any number that has been a barrier to your witness of faith. Discuss why you think this is so.

1. The Fear Barrier: "I'm afraid to witness."
2. The Perfection Barrier: "I'm not good enough to witness."
3. The Spiritual Gift Barrier: "I don't have the gift to witness."
4. The Professional Barrier: "Witnessing is the pastor's job."
5. The Model Barrier: "I'm no Billy Graham."
6. The Time Barrier: "I don't have the time to witness."
7. The Knowledge Barrier: "I don't know how to witness."
8. The Stranger Barrier: "I can't witness to strangers."
9. The Kinship-Friendship Barrier: "I'm too close to witness to them."

From *Overcoming Barriers to Witnessing* by Delos Miles. Copyright © 1984 Broadman Press. All rights reserved. Used by permission.

Read

"Give Me a W-I-T-N-E-S-S"

We often build barriers to witnessing actively for Jesus Christ because we're confused about what witnessing really is—and is not. Being a witness is not being a salesman. We aren't called to use high-pressure tactics to "win a soul." As a matter of fact, we are unable to convert anyone. That's God's job. 1 Corinthians 12:3 tells us, "No one can say 'Jesus Christ is Lord' except by the Holy Spirit."

Being a witness also does not mean we must have all the answers. Too often we shrink back from talking about God because of the "Knowledge Barrier." Jay Smith may want to start a debate with Muslims, but we sure don't! We think to ourselves, "What if they make an argument that I can't rebut? Or what if they're searching for answers to difficult questions. What will I tell them?"

In order to become more bold in witnessing, we need to change our working definition of what witnessing means. When people are called to be a witness in a court setting, it isn't assumed that they will be able to talk about all the details of the case. Neither is it the responsibility of a witness to win the case for the plaintiff or defendant. Rather, it is the job of a witness to speak truthfully concerning the things he has heard and seen. That's exactly the definition the apostle John gives regarding testifying about God: "That which was from the beginning, which we have heard, which we have seen with our eyes, which we have looked at and our hands have touched—this we proclaim concerning the Word of life" (1 John 1:1).

When we witness, we tell the story and show the love of Jesus. We tell the story of Jesus as it relates to our own story. We tell not only of the cross but also of how God's redemption through the blood of Jesus has touched our lives. We not only speak of God's forgiveness but also show God's forgiveness by extending it to others. Witnessing is more narrative than it is lecture.

Erwin J. Kolb perhaps offers the best definition of a witness by making an acrostic out of the word "witness." For Kolb, a witness is:

W   "Witness" I am a disciple of Jesus who is called to share His Good News.

I   "Intentional" Witnessing means taking the initiative to tell and show God's love with others.

T   "Testimony" Witnessing is telling Jesus' story and how it affects my own story.

N   "Natural" Witnessing becomes a part of my lifestyle and everyday conversation.

E   "Everyone" All disciples of Jesus, even I, have been made witnesses and are given opportunities to do so.

S   "Save" Because Christ came to save the lost, the goal of witnessing is to save. This is accomplished by the Holy Spirit.

S   "Some" I realize that the response to my testimony will be varied.

Adapted from *A Witness Primer*, by Erwin J. Kolb, © 1986 CPH. All rights reserved.

REACT

1. Which letters in Kolb's acrostic help you get a handle on what it means to witness your faith in Jesus?

2. Share an event in your life where Jesus' story (who He is and what He has done) intersects with your story. How has God shown His grace to you, and what impact has it had on your life?

Read

Give Me a Reason

St. Peter wrote his first epistle in Rome shortly before A.D. 64. He addresses his letter to "God's elect, strangers in the world, scattered throughout … Asia" (1 Peter 1:1). It was a time of great persecution of the Christians by the Roman emperor Nero. In these dire circumstances, Peter encourages Christians, "In your hearts set apart Christ as Lord. Always be prepared to give an answer to everyone who asks you to give the reason for the hope that you have. But do this with gentleness and respect" (1 Peter 3:15).

Peter knew that even as they faced persecution, Christians have a great opportunity to witness powerfully. Peter practiced what he preached. Instead of fleeing Nero's reign of terror, Peter stayed in Rome to testify to the truth and was ultimately apprehended. Some accounts state that when Peter was ordered to be crucified in front of thousands of spectators in the Coliseum, he requested to be crucified upside down, because he didn't feel worthy to die in the same manner as his Lord. Even in death, Peter was a witness.

The Holy Spirit working through God's Word encourages us to be prepared to give a reason for our hope. An intentional witness is prepared to talk about his or her faith. Some preparation from God's Word will enable us to verbalize our testimony so that we may better tell His story and how it relates to our story. Consider the following details:

- that God is holy and just (Isaiah 6:3; 1 Peter 1:15–16);
- that man is sinful and cannot save himself (1 John 3:8; Romans 3:23);
- that God is also a loving and merciful God (Psalm 103:10; Ephesians 2:4);
- that Jesus Christ, God's only Son, took on human flesh and died on the cross for our sins (John 3:16; John 1:14; Galatians 3:13);
- that all who believe in Jesus are made right—have a restored relationship—with God (Romans 3:21–22; Titus 2:14);

- that the Holy Spirit gives and strengthens our faith (Ephesians 2:8–9; 1 Corinthians 12:3).

God does not give the ability to verbalize faith to only missionaries and pastors. Instead the Holy Spirit gives to all of God's children an aptitude for witnessing. Once again, God, using St. Peter, provides us a stellar example. As you may recall, Peter was by trade a fisherman. On one occasion in Acts 4, he was dragged before the Jewish elders and teachers of the law in Jerusalem to defend his faith. Peter's witness took the religious leaders by surprise: "When they saw the courage of Peter and John and realized that they were unschooled, ordinary men, they were astonished"(Acts 4:13). What was Peter's reply to their amazement? "We cannot help speaking about what we have seen and heard" (v. 20).

REACT

1. Have you ever been surprised by the bold witness of an "ordinary" Christian? Share that experience.

2. Read Acts 22:1–21. How does Paul tell the story of Jesus as it relates to his own story?

Read

Actions Speak Louder

During the mid-1990s, Dave Wolter was the head women's basketball coach for Concordia University in Irvine, California. Dave is also a Christian. He had the opportunity for several summers to fly to Asia and put on some basketball clinics for both players and coaches. On one particular flight, his plane experienced mechanical trouble at 30,000 feet. Panic immediately broke out in the cabin. People were screaming, crying, and standing up in the aisles. Wolter, on the other hand, sat calmly and prayed. When one of the women sitting next to him saw how different his demeanor was to the rest of the passengers, she shouted in Wolter's face: "You are not hysterical. Why aren't you hysterical?" Fortunately, the crew was able to correct the problem, and nervous tranquillity was restored in the cabin. For the rest of the flight, Dave had the opportunity to answer the woman's question as she and several others listened intently to how his faith in Christ Jesus enables him to face death with such confidence.

Witnessing takes place not only through our words, but also through our actions. St. Peter tells us, "Live such good lives among the pagans that, though they accuse you of doing wrong, they may see your good deeds and glorify God on the day He visits us" (1 Peter 2:12). Sometimes the most powerful sermons aren't preached—they're lived. Stated another way, the fish symbol on the rear bumper of your car definitely makes a statement, but people will probably pay more attention to how you drive.

Those who witness intentionally take into account the testimony of their lives. Our lives are not meant to be detached from our faith, but rather to flow from it. Christians strive to maintain high biblical ethics to give glory to God and to bear witness to the world. "Let your light shine before men," Jesus tells us, "that they may see your good deeds and praise your Father in heaven" (Matthew 5:16).

What about those times when we've blown it—when our segment seen through other people's candid cameras doesn't look so good? We need not engage in hypocrisy, cover-ups,

64

political "spin," or excuses. Rather, in confessing our sin and seeking God's forgiveness, we teach others about grace and how God can overcome people's past mistakes and regrets. After all, what makes us Christians is not our high ethics, but the forgiveness God has provided us through Jesus' death on the cross. In short, you are called to "be wise in the way you act toward outsiders; make the most of every opportunity. Let your conversation be always full of grace, seasoned with salt, so that you may know how to answer everyone" (Colossians 4:5).

Respond

1. Look at the barriers that you circled earlier in this chapter. Choose one of them, and pray that the Holy Spirit would break it down.

2. Learn more about the reason for our hope. Enroll in a Christian instruction class, study the catechism, or check out a book from your church or Christian bookstore on witnessing. Remember, intentional witnesses are prepared to speak about the basics of Christianity.

3. Prepare your own story. Take time to reflect on how God has blessed you in your life. Describe in your own words what grace, faith, and love mean, and write your descriptions. Thank God as you recall His kindness toward you.

4. Begin to pray regularly for one to three people to whom you can witness. These may be members of your family, neighbors, teammates, or co-workers. Pray that the Holy Spirit will use you to be a living witness to them. Pray for opportunities to be able to speak about your faith as well. Pray that they will come to know Jesus Christ as Savior and Lord.

ANSWERS and COMMENTS

1
Worship:
The Most Important Hour
in Your Week

Opening

Pray together that the Lord would bless your study of His Word.

Ready

Read aloud the interview. Assign one participant the part of *Godly Man* (G.M.) and another the part of Craig Olsen.

React

1. Answers will vary.
2. Allow volunteers to share their responses. Don't force anyone to speak.

Read

"Come On!"

Read aloud the introduction to Psalm 95. Then invite volunteers to read the psalm aloud.

React

1. Verses 1 and 2 describe worship as a joyful experience. In worship we come before the Lord with joy and thanksgiving, praising Him with music and song. Answers will vary to

the second question. Move the discussion along. Don't let this question become the basis for a "gripe session."

2. The psalmist says we worship God for He is a great king, the Creator, who cares for us. Invite participants to give reasons for worshiping God. In worship God speaks to us in His Word.

3. Answers will vary.

Read

But I'll Miss Sunday Morning Football!

Read aloud or invite volunteers to read this section aloud.

React

1. Answers will vary. It is likely that participants have either known a "Mike Holmgren" or been him at some point in their lives.

2. Anything or anyone that becomes first in our lives is a "god." These gods come in all shapes and sizes. They may include sports, job, alcohol, sex, and so forth.

Read

Worship or Whine?

Read aloud this section. Ask, "When is it easiest for you to praise God?" Allow time for participants to respond. Have volunteers read aloud Exodus 17:1–7 as printed in the Study Guide.

React

1. The Israelites complained because they had no water to drink. In Israel the people were not only thirsty but also hungry and persecuted.

2. The people of Israel questioned whether God was really with them.

3. Answers will vary. Trials can cause us to question God

and His presence and His care in our lives. God can and does use trials to draw us closer to Him. When we realize that we are helpless on our own to control situations, we can remember God's promise to be with us always.

4. Answers will vary. Urge participants to share people who have continued to worship God even as they faced suffering and trials.

Read

No Worship, No Rest

Invite volunteers to read aloud this section. Discuss the concept of a "hardened" heart. Ask, "What could cause a person to harden his heart? What is the danger of a heart hardened to God and His Word?"

Respond

Read through the suggested activities. Urge participants to complete one or more before the next time you meet.

Closing

Pray together that God will make worship a number 1 priority in your lives.

2
Being a Spiritual Leader at Home

Opening

Pray together that, as your faith is strengthened by the power of the Holy Spirit working through God's Word, you will be empowered to be spiritual leaders in your homes.

Ready

Read aloud the opening paragraph. Then allow time for participants to work independently to complete the activity.

React

Allow time for participants to share their responses to the "Ready" activity with other members of the group.

1. Answers will vary.

2. Again, responses will vary.

3. Most men have had a role model. Urge participants to share the name of their role model(s) and the reason this person was such a strong model.

Read

Me, a Spiritual Leader?

Read aloud or invite volunteers to read aloud this rather lengthy section.

React

1. Allow participants to share their memories of the spiritual leadership their fathers provided.

2. Allow time for participants to respond.

Read

A Guy Named Eli

Read aloud the opening paragraph. Then have volunteers read aloud 1 Samuel 3:2–18.

React

1. God's judgment on Eli may seem extreme to some. A priest may neglect spiritual leadership in the home as he concerns himself with the busyness of his job. Spiritual leadership may be difficult for men for many different reasons: lack of role model in the home, lack of time, busyness on the job, and so forth.

2. Answers will vary. Allow time for participants to share how they might positively influence the faith development of their children. Answers may include spending time with them, praying with them, taking them to worship, and having family devotions.

3. God desires the man to provide spiritual leadership to the family.

Read

Taking the Right Passage

Read aloud this section concerning the lack of spiritual leadership exercised by men in their homes and how men might better demonstrate spiritual leadership.

Respond

Read aloud the introductory paragraphs to this section. Then urge participants to complete the suggested activity during the following week.

Closing

Invite participants to share concerns, joys, and sorrows that they wish to bring to God in prayer. Then if participants feel comfortable doing so, invite them to pray for these concerns. Close the prayer by thanking God for allowing you to be the spiritual leader in your home.

3
Real Men Pray

Opening

Pray together that the Holy Spirit will strengthen your faith through the study of God's Word and in so doing enable you to pray more boldly and more often.

Ready

Read aloud the introductory paragraphs. Then invite volunteers to read the portion of *Piercing the Darkness*.

Read

Take a Breather!

Read aloud the opening paragraphs. Then invite volunteers to read aloud Daniel 6:1–23.

React

1. Daniel prayed three times a day. Daniel gave thanks to God.

2. Answers will vary. If honest, some men will admit that they would hide or even stop praying if they were threatened with persecution. Remind participants that Jesus went to the cross to earn for us forgiveness for the times when our fear causes us to reject and/or deny our faith.

3. Answers will vary.

Read

Of First Importance

Ask, "Is prayer sometimes a last resort for you as you

face difficult trials or temptations?" Allow time for participants to respond. Then read aloud or invite volunteers to read aloud this section.

Read

Sometimes It's the Only Solution

Read aloud this section. Then invite volunteers to read aloud Exodus 17:8–16.

React

1. Although it may not have seemed wise to keep Moses and Aaron out of the battle, the very lives of the soldiers depended upon it. For through the prayers of Moses, the victory was won.

2. As Moses' hands remained lifted in prayer, the soldiers were successful in battle.

3. Aaron assisted Moses by helping to keep his hands raised in prayer.

4. Answers will vary.

Read

Where Do I Start?

Read aloud the opening section. Then read together the Lord's Prayer from Luke 11:1–4 printed in the Study Guide.

Read

Jesus' Prayer

Read aloud the explanation of the Lord's Prayer.

Read and React

Jesus' Prayer Life

Have participants complete the activity independently. Then discuss their responses.

Read

Jesus Makes Prayer Work

Read aloud or invite volunteers to read aloud this section.

Respond

Read through the suggested activities. Then urge participants to complete one or more of the suggested activities prior to the next time you meet.

Closing

Invite participants to share prayer concerns. List these concerns on a sheet of newsprint or on a chalkboard. Then ask volunteers to pray for these concerns. Close by praying together the Lord's Prayer.

4

Strengthening and Supporting One Another

Ready

Read aloud this scenario.

React

1. Answers will vary.
2. Answers will vary.
3. Again, responses to the question will vary.

Read

A Story on Strengthening

Read aloud the opening section. Then invite volunteers to read aloud the Parable of the Good Samaritan found in Luke 10:30–37.

React

1. Answers will vary. As in Jesus' day, there are people in our society who have experienced rejection and persecution.
2. When Christians shirk their responsibility to love, they fail to give a positive witness to their faith.
3. Answers will vary.

Read

No "I" in Body

Read aloud the introductory paragraphs in this section.

Then invite volunteers to read aloud 1 Corinthians 12:12–27.

Read

Give Them Bread This Day

Emphasize the fact that God calls us into His family through Holy Baptism. Read aloud this section.

React

1. Paul's teaching does in fact challenge the prevailing "meism" evident in today's society. Answers will vary to the second question.

2. People feel disconnected from the body of Christ, when they believe they don't need to be a part of the body and when they believe that they don't need the other members of the body. Answers to the second question will vary.

3. Answers will vary. Again, see this question as an opportunity to discuss concerns and look for solutions. This question should not turn into an opportunity for participants to gripe.

4. Answers will vary.

Read

The Full Extent of God's Love

Read aloud the opening paragraph. Then invite a volunteer to read John 13:1–17.

Read

How Do You Spell "Servant"?

Read this section aloud. Emphasize the servant role Jesus took when He willingly went to the cross to suffer and die for our sins.

Respond

Read through the suggested activities. Then urge participants to complete one or more before the next time you meet.

Closing

Close this session by thanking God for the relationship He restored between Himself and us through His Son's death on the cross. Pray that by the Spirit's power you will demonstrate Jesus' love to others during the coming week.

5
Honoring God with Time, Talents, and Treasures

Ready

Read aloud the opening paragraphs. Then allow time for participants to complete a pie chart independently. Ask for volunteers to share their completed pie charts with the rest of the group.

Read

It's about Time

Invite volunteers to read aloud this section.

Read

The Time Is Right

Ask for volunteers to read aloud the Parable of the Great Banquet found in Luke 14:15–24.

React

1. The invited guests were preoccupied with all sorts of excuses: "I have just bought a field." "I have just bought five yoke of oxen." "I just got married." Answers to the second question will vary.

2. "When the time had fully come, God sent His Son, born of a woman, born under law, to redeem those under law." We

receive the full rights of sons and daughters of God through Jesus' death on the cross. God's timing for our salvation motivates us to use our time to give God glory.

3. Answers will vary.

Read

Show Talent

Read about God's gift of talents. Then invite a volunteer to read aloud the Parable of the Talents found in Matthew 25:14–30.

React

1. The third man was afraid of the master. Answers to the second question will vary.

2. Provide ample time for volunteers to share.

Read

You're the Man for the Job!

Read aloud or invite volunteers to read aloud portions of this section.

Read

Gimme!

Read the introductory paragraph to this section on treasures. Then invite a volunteer to read aloud the Parable of the Rich Fool in Luke 12:13–21.

React

1. God accused the rich man of being a fool because he spent his life storing up riches instead of pursuing that which would provide Him eternal life—his faith relationship with God.

2. Allow time for participants to share how they have at times foolishly used the treasures God has provided them.

3. Through His Word God enables us to be rich toward Him (and others). The Holy Spirit works through God's Word to create saving faith and to strengthen that faith.

Read

Owner or Manager?

Invite volunteers to read aloud this rather lengthy section that compares the concept of owner to manager.

React

1. Have participants place an "X" on the continuum to describe their giving as *to* or *from*. Allow time for volunteers to share the reason for their responses.

2. Answers will vary.

3. God's love for us in Christ motivates us to give richly to Him.

Respond

Read through the suggested activities. Then urge participants to complete one or more of the activities prior to the next time the group meets.

Closing

Confess your sinful use of the time, talents, and treasures God has given you. Assure the members of the group of the forgiveness Jesus won for them on the cross. Pray that God's love for them in Christ will enable and empower them to use their time, talents, and treasures to His glory.

6
Living a Life of Witness

Opening

Pray that through the study of God's Word today, the Holy Spirit will strengthen your faith so that you might witness boldly and effectively God's love for you in Christ Jesus.

Ready

Read the story of Jay Smith a missionary to the Muslims in England.

React

1. Although answers will vary, typically confronting a friend or loved is not considered the most effective way to witness our faith in Christ Jesus.

2. Answers will vary.

Read

To Be or Not to Be ... a Witness

Read aloud the opening paragraphs. Emphasize that, by virtue of the fact that God in His mercy and grace has called us to faith, we are witnesses.

React

Read aloud the opening paragraph. Then invite a different participant to read aloud each of the barriers. Ask,

"What is the greatest barrier you face in witnessing your faith to friends and loved ones?" Allow time for volunteers to share.

Read

"Give Me a W-I-T-N-E-S-S"

Read aloud or invite volunteers to read this section. Have a different participant read aloud each of the portions of the witness definition developed by Kolb.

React

1. Answers will vary.

2. Allow ample time for volunteers to share their stories and how God has intersected their stories. This activity will provide practice for participants in witnessing their faith.

Read

Give Me a Reason

Read aloud this section that describes St. Peter's witness of faith. Then spend time going through the details of Jesus' story. Suggest that participants memorize these details so that they can use them when God provides them new opportunities to witness their faith. Urge participants to practice sharing these details during the weeks that follow.

React

1. Answers will vary.

2. Paul tells how Jesus intervened in his life, transforming him from one who persecuted Christians to a powerful witness of the Gospel. Through God's Word the Holy Spirit transforms our lives, enabling us to witness boldly our faith in Christ Jesus.

Read

Actions Speak Louder

Ask, "How do actions sometimes speak louder than words?" Allow a few volunteers to share. Then read aloud the story of David Wolter.

Respond

Review each of the suggested activities. Then urge participants to complete one or more of the activities during the coming weeks.

Closing

Pray that the Holy Spirit will enable you to witness boldly your faith in Christ Jesus.